STILL LEARNING

A 50 YEAR HISTORY OF
MONASH UNIVERSITY PENINSULA CAMPUS

Fay Woodhouse

ACKNOWLEDGEMENTS

I would like to acknowledge the generous assistance in both time and documentary material – archives, photographs and stories – provided to me by many current and past members of staff. Professor Phillip Steele, Ms Sue Webb, Ms Tanya O'Brien and Ms Melinda Robinson have all contributed to the task of documenting Monash Peninsula Campus' history. Former staff members, too, have been generous with their time, and I thank especially Bob Greaves and Kate Boyle. I thank the former students I have spoken to including Max Gillies, Peter Corlett and Paul Jennings.

Writing such a history as this would not have been possible without the assistance and enthusiasm of archival and library staff, and I sincerely thank Monash Peninsula Library including Paula Todd and staff, and Monash University Archives staff, particularly Jan Getson and Lyn Maloney. Finally, I would like to acknowledge the expertise of editor Tracy Jennings and indexer Jane Purton and thank them for their exemplary work.

Fay Woodhouse

STILL LEARNING

A 50 YEAR HISTORY OF MONASH UNIVERSITY PENINSULA CAMPUS

By Fay Woodhouse

CONTENTS

Chapter		Page
Foreword		4
1.	Introduction	5
2.	Frankston by-the-sea: Pre-history and early settlement	7
3.	Frankston Teachers' College – 1959 to 1973	9
4.	The first transition: From Teachers' College to State College of Victoria at Frankston – 1974 to 1982	18
5.	Amalgamation challenges: Chisholm Institute of Technology – 1982 to 1990	25
6.	And now we are Monash University	30
7.	Conclusion	40
References		42
Index		44

FOREWORD

I am delighted to introduce *Still Learning: A 50 Year History of Monash University Peninsula Campus* authored by Dr Fay Woodhouse, which outlines the development of the campus since its establishment in 1958.

The Monash Peninsula Campus has a proud and rich history reflecting an ongoing commitment to post-secondary education and to serving the needs of its local community. The campus has played a variety of roles as the Frankston Teachers' College, a college of the State College Victoria, the Frankston campus of the Chisholm Institute of Technology and most recently as the Peninsula Campus of Monash University.

Monash University is also celebrating its 50th Anniversary this year, with the statute establishing the university being approved by the Victorian Parliament in 1958. Although 50 years is a very short period of time in the life of a great university, Monash has made remarkable progress in becoming a leading Australian university.

Since its establishment, the Monash Peninsula Campus has embraced a strong commitment to the education of teachers, which remains a major focus to this day. However, over the years the academic program has been broadened substantially with three faculties now undertaking teaching and research at the campus: Business and Economics, Education, and Medicine, Nursing and Health Sciences.

The Peninsula Campus now plays a unique and valuable role in the life of Monash University. Over recent years the campus has developed an academic theme embracing health and wellbeing involving teaching and research in physiotherapy, occupational therapy, health science, nursing and midwifery, sport and outdoor recreation, early childhood and primary education and business and economics.

I would like to acknowledge the wonderful contribution of all previous and existing staff members and students who have made the campus the very special learning community that it is today.

Philip Steele
Pro Vice-Chancellor Campus Coordination
Academic Director Berwick and Peninsula
Monash University

1. INTRODUCTION

The site of the Monash University Peninsula Campus has been an educational institution for 50 years. The impact of the post-War baby boom and immigration policy saw increased enrolments at primary schools across Victoria and demand for teachers outweighed supply. The Education Department responded to the increased need and in 1958 two new teachers colleges were established. Frankston Teachers' College opened its doors in 1959 with an enrolment of 109 students. 1958 also marked the establishment and incorporation of 'a University to be known as Monash University' (*Monash University Act* 1958 No. 6184), located in the outer Melbourne suburb of Clayton. Though staff and students from Frankston crossed educational paths with Monash from the outset, it would be 32 years and several mergers of educational institutions later, before the current Monash University Peninsula Campus was formed.

Increases in population and a more affluent society, together with greater demands for higher or advanced education, led to several government inquiries into the higher education sector from the 1970s. The Education Department relinquished control over the States' Teacher Training Colleges, and in 1972, Frankston was one of six colleges which formed the State College of Victoria (SCV). In 1982 the State College of Victoria at Frankston amalgamated with the Caulfield Institute of Technology to form the Chisholm Institute of Technology. Frankston became one of its two campuses and remained so until 1990 when that institution merged with Monash University to become Monash University Peninsula Campus.

From its first days, the local community were considered a significant part of the Frankston Teachers' College. Parents of local students formed the Welfare Association for the provision of amenities to the College and for the promotion and development of public relations between the College and community generally. During its time as the State College of Victoria at Frankston, community engagement broadened with invitations extended to groups representing local government, migrants, service organisations and community workers in order to meet members of the Council and staff. Additionally, evening classes and lectures were offered for members of the local community, continuing under the banner of the Chisholm Institute of Technology. Since 1990, when Chisholm merged with the rapidly growing Monash University, connections to the community have increased even further.

With its expansion of courses, the Peninsula Campus now attracts students from suburbs across Melbourne as well as from the extremity of the Mornington Peninsula and from across the world. After 18 years as one of Monash University's suburban campuses, Peninsula has clearly created a niche for itself within the multi-campus Monash network and built upon the existing strong links with its local community.

Figure 1 The Education Building
Photographer: Melissa Diciero, Advancement, Monash University

2. FRANKSTON BY-THE-SEA: PRE-HISTORY AND EARLY SETTLEMENT

The traditional owners of the Frankston area were the Bunurong people, part of the language group or nation known as Koolin, sometimes spelt, Kulin. They claim land from the Werribee River to Wilson's Promontory in the south-east, taking in the catchments of the old Carrum Swamp, Westernport Bay including the Mornington Peninsula, Phillip Island, French Island and the Tarwin River (Compton, 2008). One of the clans of the Bunurong, the Mayone Bulluk Bunurong, lived in coastal camps at Mordialloc, Frankston and Warneet on Westernport Bay (City of Greater Dandenong, 2008). Through the summer they collected kangaroo and possum skins for winter clothes. In the winter months they moved inland where they caught eels, collected shoots and mushrooms, and seeds from ant's nests. Middens on the cliff tops of the Mornington Peninsula indicate that the Bunurong Aborigines used the area on a seasonal basis for hundreds if not thousands of years before the arrival of Europeans.

The Bunurong's first encounter with Europeans probably dates back to the sighting of the French ship *l'Astrolabe*. Its commander, Dumont d'Urville, recorded a visit to Westernport Bay in his diary in 1826. He notes sighting sealers, their Aboriginal wives and children. The first sighting was recorded by lithographer Hippolyte Vanderburch, on board *l'Astrolabe*.

European settlement was formalised after 1835 when the District of Port Phillip was opened up to squatters wishing to graze their cattle and sheep. The whole district was divided into Parishes and the first parish plans were drawn up. In 1851 the district of Port Phillip separated from New South Wales and became the Colony of Victoria. Surveying and land sales in Victoria continued with the influx of migrants in search of gold and merchants ready to supply their needs.

Frankston was first known as a fishing village 26 miles (40 kms) from Melbourne. The fishermen sailed up to Melbourne to sell their catch or travelled along the 'Fish Track' which later served as the basis of the Nepean Highway. The first school was established in 1855, the first Frankston post office was opened in 1857, and in the same year a pier was completed. By the 1860s, Frankston's population was around 30 residents with about 200 in the surrounding area. The first state school was built in Frankston in 1874; a Mechanics' Institute and free library were constructed in 1880.

The first savings bank opened in 1881, and when the railway arrived in 1882, Frankston gradually became a popular holiday resort. William M K Vale purchased 320 acres of crown land at Frankston after declaring that, with its picturesque scenery, Frankston and Snapper's Point were 'likely to become the Ramsgate of Victoria and certainly the rival of Queenscliff' (Inglis, 1999: 5). Following Federation in 1901, Frankston developed slowly, first as a seaside resort and fishing village and later as a small regional township. It was declared a city in 1966.

3. FRANKSTON TEACHERS' COLLEGE – 1959 TO 1973

THE SITE AT FRANKSTON – A HOUSE NAMED *STRUAN*

The land on which Monash University's Peninsula Campus was built is first mentioned in the Frankston rate books of 1896–7. The land was owned by Mrs Jane Unthank, a local identity. The property was subdivided and changed hands three times before being purchased by Mr Rudolph Werner of Richmond in 1920. A new house was constructed in 1924 in the Edwardian Arts and Crafts style, popular in the 1920s. Werner owned the house until his death when it passed from his estate to Escort Rudolph Werner on 16 February 1945. The title then consisted of 17.5 acres.

Dr Frank R Vincent purchased the house and land from Werner's estate in January 1951 and named the property *Struan*. Dr Vincent, who worked at the nearby Frankston Hospital, owned and occupied the site until he offered it for sale to the Education Department in 1957.

POST-WAR MIGRATION, THE BABY BOOM AND THE NEED FOR MORE TEACHERS

R J W Selleck, education historian argues that post-war forces, especially the migration policy which contributed to the population explosion of the late 1940s and 1950s, changed Australian education drastically (Selleck 1998: 205). Don Garden (1982: 181) also notes that the 1950s and 1960s 'saw an enormous growth in the Victorian education system' because of the Commonwealth immigration schemes, the affluence of the community and the mounting demand for higher qualifications. The post-War baby boom had its greatest impact between 1951 and 1961 when the number of Victorian primary school pupils increased from 205,888 to 301,514 (181). The demand for teachers overtook supply; the Education Department was unable to produce enough teachers. Classrooms, sometimes with up to sixty students, were full to overflowing. Something had to be done quickly and it was this overcrowding that the Education Department acknowledged.

In response to the demand for primary teachers, in 1958 Coburg College was planned for the north-west of Melbourne and Frankston was chosen as the location for a college in the south-eastern suburbs. This location was chosen because of the availability of training schools in the area, the likely enrolment of students from the area, the distance from the railway, and the possibility of improving and developing the site. Consequently, after some negotiation, the Education Department took up Dr Vincent's offer of his property which consisted of an 11-roomed house and a 4-roomed cottage set within 17 acres, 3 roods and 27 perches of land on the corner of McMahons and Hastings Road (Monash University Archives). The property was acquired on 8 October 1957 for £37,500.

A further seven properties were acquired at an additional cost of £18,316, making a total purchase price of £55,816 (Monash University Archives).

FIRST APPOINTMENTS 1958

Advertisements for the first Frankston Teachers' College positions were placed in the *Education Gazette and Teachers' Aid* on 22 May 1958. They were for the positions of: Principal, Lecturer Grade 1 (man) Lecturer Grade 1 (woman) and two positions as Lecturer Grade 3 (man or woman).

On 24 July 1958, Mr Warwick Eunson, BA, B.Ed., TPTC, Lib. Reg., then lecturer at the Melbourne Teachers' College (MTC), was appointed Principal of the newly created Frankston Teachers' College under the *Teaching Service Act* 1946. His annual salary was set at a rate of £1675 per annum (VPRS10536/P/0000 Unit 19).

The first four appointments to lecturing positions were made on 17 October 1958; they were Alwyn H Fry of Burwood Teachers' College, Gertrude F Kentish of Geelong Teachers' College, Thomas J Dignam of Toorak Teachers' College, and George W D Boyd of Bendigo Teachers' College. The male Lecturer Grade 1 position earned an annual salary of £1550; for Lecturer Grade 3 the rate was £1320–1550, while the salary for a female Lecturer Grade 1, £1320, reflected the policy of paying women around two-thirds of the male wage. Women were also required to resign from the Education Department when they married, though by the 1960s they were enticed back into the classroom because of the high demand.

The 11-room house, *Struan*, was quickly adapted to become lecture rooms, staff rooms, offices and a library. Plans were made to build a college from the ground up.

A COLLEGE IS CREATED

On 1 January 1959, Warwick Eunson and his nine staff members officially began working for Frankston Teachers' College. In just six weeks, Eunson and his staff had finalised the curriculum and timetables and negotiated teaching rounds at the chosen local schools. Quite a feat in such a short space of time! On 12 February they welcomed their first 109 students.

The excitement of the new venture for both staff and students can still be felt across the distance of nearly 50 years. Archival documents, newsletters and the student publication, *Struan*, record this excitement. The Principal produced a pamphlet which was given to each student on their first day. Simply titled, *Information for Students 1959*, it formed his official opening address to both students and staff. Here he spelled out the situation the new college faced:

> This little booklet is planned to welcome you to the college ... You have joined this year a group of some 1,400 young people like yourselves, beginning this year in Teachers' Colleges at Melbourne, Toorak, Burwood, Geelong, Bendigo or Ballarat, all well-established colleges, or in the two new colleges at Coburg and your own Frankston. It is a great adventure to be in "at the start" of a new institution, and to help build its traditions. Your staff feel this way about this college, and ask you to join them in this task, so that you will be proud to say "I trained at Frankston."

Eunson went on: conditions were far from ideal because of the limited space, extra-curricular activities such as sport were as much part of the experience as study, and these activities were in the hands of the Student Representative Council (SRC). Lecture timetables were set out, details of the five training schools the students would later teach at were documented, the date of fortnightly payments was provided, as well as hints on dress and behaviour. These were formal times; men were addressed as 'Mr' and women as 'Miss'. Former staff members also recall that men were discouraged from wearing a beard and women should not wear red!

As the year progressed, both staff and students were actively engrossed in the College and their work. An emblem, the Seahorse, was chosen for the college. This emblem has endured and remains part of the fabric of the University, commemorated in the naming of the Seahorse Tavern. By May design and tender documents for the construction of a new building were advertised and construction began mid-year. In December 1959, a college Welfare Association was inaugurated following a meeting of 200 parents and citizens. It was the first association of its kind connected with a Victorian teachers' college (*Struan*, 1960: 22).

Figure 2 Seahorse
Monash University Archives, MON 1206 Frankston Teachers' College Yearbooks

One aspect of working as a teacher in Victoria was the right to become part of a teachers' union. The Victorian Teachers' Union was established in 1926 with a membership of around 5000. In 1946 the VTU established the Victorian Teachers' Tribunal whose purpose was to fix wages, salaries and general conditions of employment. In 1948 the secondary teachers broke away and in 1953 formed the Victorian Secondary Teachers' Association (VSTA). In 1959, the Victorian Teachers' Union (VTU) was by far the largest and most influential professional teaching association in Victoria. An article advertising the Union in the 1961 *Handbook* advised that the Union then had 16,000 members and that 100% of staff and the present second year students at Frankston belonged to this Union. Of the 76 graduating students of 1960, 75 elected to join the union.

The *Teachers' College Handbook 1960* reported on the College's first year of operation. Courses available at Frankston from 1959–78 were the Trained Primary Teachers' Certificate (TPTC) and Trained Infant Teachers' Certificate (TITC) (available only to women). Successful completion of these courses enabled students to be selected for courses in specialised teaching, such as the Trained Special Teachers' Certificate, Art and Craft Teachers' Certificate (Primary), Teacher-Librarian's Certificate, Home Crafts Certificate or, for selection to the Secondary Teachers' College at the University of Melbourne. Entry into this course also enabled students to enter the University.

Figure 3 First students and teacher outside *Struan*, 1959
Monash University Archives, MON 1026, Frankston Teachers' College Yearbooks

Classroom training was an essential part of the course, and training schools accessible to the college increased from 5 in 1959 to 14 in 1960. After only one year of operation, both teaching staff and enrolments at Frankston more than doubled, from 24 and 252 respectively; this pattern of growth continued for the next twelve years. Frankston Teachers' College was growing in leaps and bounds. In December 1960, the first graduation ceremony took place.

STUDENT LIFE 1959

Accepting a teaching bursary in 1959 from the Education Department and a place at one of the six teaching colleges meant students were bonded to teach in the Victorian State Education system for three years. While conscious of their commitment to the Education Department and other possibilities available to them, student life, as Warwick Eunson and subsequent Principals insisted, meant more than study. In 1959, a Student Representative Council (SRC) was elected. *Struan,* a student publication, was inaugurated and editors elected. The magazine was published at the end of each year prior to the summer break.

The first edition of *Struan,* published in 1960, documents the College's first year. The editor, Peter Hart, the Principal, staff and students, all contributed to the first edition. The editor reported on the formation of the first SRC, progress on the construction of the first building, social functions – including the 'Miss Frankston Teachers' College' award – the music club, library club, 'Fossickers Club', a trip to Central Australia and other events. The magazine also included poetry, reviews of sporting activities, and reflections on a teaching round. Reading the first and subsequent editions of *Struan* conveys a strong sense of community within the Teachers' College: this sense of community is palpable through the words and the images on the page.

The 1950s and early 1960s, coming as they did before the storm of student protests and activism of the late 1960s and 1970s, are often seen as a period of student conformism and quiescence. The 1954–5 Labour Party split had devastated the Australian political landscape and in 1960 the Cold War was still heating up. Some of the students at Frankston Teachers' College were worried by government censorship of teaching and literary journals as well as novels and films. While groundbreaking research into children's learning frequently appeared in educational journals from the United States and the UK, some of these were censored documents and government permission was required to access them.

In the 1960s Vladimir Nabokov's novel, *Lolita* and D H Lawrence's *Lady Chatterley's Lover* were banned by the Australian government; these censorship laws were addressed by a student, Margaret Reynolds, in her *Struan* article entitled 'Censorship':

> In a country which values freedom of speech, the banning of any book, even the most obscene, is a direct blow against that liberty to express any opinion. Intellectual liberty and artistic liberty are mere empty phrases while the censor stands between the writer and his public (*Struan*, 1961: 4).

This particular article was not censored by the printer. However, as the editor, Max Gillies pointed out four articles, to be published in February 1962 – 'The real world of kids', 'Humour in the classroom', 'A view to death' and one poem were substantially altered or deleted by the printing company, Standard Newspapers Ltd. In the final proof of the magazine, the printer left one page blank which enabled Gillies to attach a supplement outlining the exclusions from the original article. E J Trait, Governing Director and editor of Standard Newspapers, wrote indignantly to the Director of Education explaining that 'two items were deleted by us because of their blatant obscenity'. He continued:

> We appreciate the fact that University students publish matter sometimes which is "blue" but we felt when handling "STRUAN" that coming from a seat of learning where adolescents were being trained to be teachers, obscenity and blasphemy should not be featured. After all, these people are training to be teachers, and the minds of little children will be under their control. Those at Frankston who are responsible for this type of journalism are quite unfitted for the task. I am sure you will heartily agree with the view (VPRS 10536/P/0000 Unit 19).

Correspondence continued for a couple of weeks, until Trait backed down. In the meantime, Gillies was called before the Principal of the College and the Director of Education. He recently reflected upon the incident, saying that, while he was aware the Director General theoretically had the ability to exercise his power over Gillies' career as a teacher, 'I argued my point and stuck to my guns' (Gillies, 27 April 2008).

Max Gillies, AM

It seems Max Gillies, actor and satirist, grew up with a passion for drama. He won four prizes for his extra-curricular activities at Melbourne High, including the Drama Prize. He attended Frankston Teachers' College 1960–61, graduating with a Primary Teacher Training Certificate. At Frankston he revelled in revues and is remembered by former students for his antics. Monty Brown, who taught literature and his wife Margaret who taught drama at Frankston, stood out for Max as inspirational teachers. Max entered Monash University in 1965, graduating Bachelor of Arts (Education) 1968. He then taught history and drama at the Secondary Teachers College at the University of Melbourne. By the late 1960s Drama was the largest department at the College with more than 300 students. The teaching, he believes, was pioneering the academic field of teaching drama to student teachers and was, to some extent, the progenitor of the now long established acting and drama courses at the Victorian College of the Arts.

While he enjoyed teaching, Max made a conscious decision to earn his living as an actor, and was part of the group of ex-Monash and ex-Melbourne students who formed the La Mama Theatre in Carlton in the late 1960s; he was a founding member of the Australian Performing Group, active throughout the 1970s. He appeared as Metcalfe in the 1974 Peter Weir film, *The Cars that Ate Paris*.

Max is renowned for his television satires *The Gillies Report*, *Gillies Republic* and *Gillies and Company*. He is also renowned for his characterisations of former Australian prime ministers John Howard and Robert Menzies, Australian politicians Alexander Downer and Amanda Vanstone, former premiers Neville Wran and Joh Bjelke-Peterson, and Australian writers Phillip Adams and Geoffrey Blainey.

He became a Member of the Order of Australia in 1990 for service to the performing arts.

In 2007 he joined the University of Melbourne as a Vice-Chancellor's Fellow where, amongst other pursuits, he will assist with the development of theatre skills and practice at Parkville campus.

BUILDING A PLACE IN THE LOCAL COMMUNITY

The ongoing business of teaching and attracting new students continued under the leadership of Warwick Eunson until 1962 when he was appointed to the role of Vice Principal at Melbourne Teachers' College. In the same year the newly constructed student Hostel (built 1961) was occupied by 120 students and plans for the extension of the College were underway. Student enrolment had escalated to a staggering 425 with 34 staff – a more than three-fold increase of both students and staff since 1959. Construction of the lecture block and physical education blocks were also underway in 1962.

A new Principal, George A Jenkins, BA, BCom., BEd., MACE, TPTC, was appointed Frankston Teachers' Colleges Principal in 1963. He took over the leadership of the college, and saw student numbers increase from 425 in 1962 to 750 prior to the College's new status as State College of Victoria at Frankston in 1973. At the same time, staff numbers had increased from 34 in 1962 to 69 in 1970. The courses offered were TITC and TPTC. Jenkins is commemorated in the naming of the George Jenkins Theatre.

The new Principal, in his Foreword to the 1963 *Handbook*, continued Eunson's theme of reminding students that their experiences at Teachers' College would be 'many-sided' and advised that 'perhaps the greatest challenge faced by students entering a tertiary college was to 'use their freedom wisely' (*Handbook* 1963: 1).

During the decade 1963–72, primary teaching colleges introduced a three-year Diploma of Teaching (Primary) and the TPTC and TITC courses were phased out. In 1967, writing in the student magazine, *Struan*, Jenkins heralded changes to the College that included the new three-year TITC course with its provision for major and sub-major subjects and time for independent reading and study. Other changes were occurring; teachers were to be given time to prepare lessons during the school day, and there was to be less emphasis on assessment of teaching and more on guidance and advice. This marked the beginning of a review of the teaching program by the College's Advisory Committee. The 1967 edition of *Struan* reviewed the year, showcasing student creativity, and contained poetry, short stories, reviews of the musical theatre productions staged during the year, sporting events, art and literary awards.

Warwick Eunson (1907–83)

Raised in Northcote and educated at the University of Melbourne, after service as a junior teacher, Warwick Eunson was a student at Melbourne Teachers' College (MTC) 1928–9. He taught in a variety of schools until training as a librarian in 1946, after which he was appointed to MTC in 1947 as Librarian. He served in that capacity until appointed founding Principal of the Frankston Teachers' College in 1959. In 1962 Eunson was appointed Vice Principal of the College, a position he retained until his retirement at the end of 1965. Eunson was in charge of the College during the difficult period in the 1960s when great changes were taking place in tertiary institutions and there was great pressure on college principals. Quiet, gentlemanly and a capable administrator, he rode out the difficult years, making concessions to changing times where necessary and preserving valuable traditions and ideals where possible.

The first library at the Frankston Campus of Chisholm Institute of Technology was named in honour of Warwick Eunson. His service to libraries included membership of the first Free

Library Service Board of Victoria and Chairman of the Advisory Committee on Teachers' College Libraries (1968–72). He was foundation Registrar of the State College of Victoria and author of *The Unfolding Hills: Mirboo Pioneers of the Gippsland Forests 1878–1941*, published by Mirboo Shire Council 1978.

Figure 4 Warwick Eunson, Principal 1959-62
Monash University Archives, MON 1206, Frankston Teachers' College Yearbooks

The College was changing physically by 1972. Landscaping and planting of native trees and shrubs began to transform the Frankston site. A small area of original bushland was preserved and enclosed as a native flora and fauna reserve, named 'Yarriambiack'. A large sculpture by Art Lecturer, Owen Piggott, in Mt Gambier stone was created and placed at a focal point between the College and the Hostel; and a welded-metal wall sculpture by Ted Moran was placed at the College entrance. These sculptures, Jenkins believed, symbolised the opportunities offered by the College for students to work creatively and take an active part in the many-sided student life (*Handbook 1972*: 1).

4. THE FIRST TRANSITION: FROM TEACHERS' COLLEGE TO STATE COLLEGE OF VICTORIA AT FRANKSTON – 1974 TO 1982

The State Government of Victoria under the leadership of Liberal Premier, Sir Henry Bolte, passed the *State College of Victoria Act 1972*.

This was followed by an Order of Council effective 1 August 1973 constituting the State College of Victoria at Frankston. The new name and status of the College first appeared on the annual *Handbook* in 1974.

Following the retirement due to ill health of George Jenkins, a new Principal, Douglas Watson BA, B.Ed, TPTC, MACE, was appointed. He became the first principal of the new autonomous college in 1974. During Jenkins' period as Principal, the two-year course for the Trained Primary Teachers' Certificate and the three-year course for the Trained Infant Teachers' Certificate were replaced by the Diploma of Teaching (Primary). In 1974 enrolment at the new State College of Victoria at Frankston was 900.

An extensive building program had begun in 1972 enlarging and improving facilities at Frankston. Twin four-storey tower blocks provided a new library and resource centre, student lounge and cafeteria, staff lounge and dining area. Offices and lecture rooms for Education, English and Mathematics were opened in 1974.

Figure 5 Frankston *Icarus* Sculpture 1972
Monash University Archives, MON 1206, State College of Victoria Frankston Yearbooks

One major event of 1973 was the opening of the new theatre, library and student union. In his opening address, Education Minister and Deputy Premier, Lindsay Thompson declared that Frankston Teachers' College had made a magnificent contribution to schools in south-east Melbourne, the peninsula and Gippsland and predicted growth in the future. The theatre, named after George Jenkins, was conceived by George Pappas, who saw it as a major teaching space for dramatic arts. That dream was never realised, however, the George Jenkins Theatre did fulfil a community role as, at the time, there was no other theatre facility available in the Frankston area. In the turbulent year of 1975, politics came to the campus when a request was made to the College for the George Jenkins Theatre to be made available for a meeting to discuss the constitutional crisis. After considerable discussion, Council agreed that the theatre should be available to any outside organisation (Council Minutes, 28 November 1975).

Early in the College's life as the State College of Victoria at Frankston, Australia experienced perhaps one of its most disturbing years, both socially and politically: it was the year 1975. This was a turbulent year for the Australian population – it was also reflected by a degree of unrest experienced by the students at the State College.

A part of the place – the Portsea Annexe

The Frankston Teachers' College Annexe at Portsea was a disused rural school set on a three-acre site. It was transferred to the College by the Education Department in 1968 for development as a College camp. The first camp was enjoyed by students and teachers in 1969.

The College utilised the Annexe at Portsea because they saw it as an opportunity for expanding the cultural and social experiences of students by transferring them from the formalised environment of the College to the informal, natural environment of the bushland setting. All students spent one week at the Annexe during their first year of study.

Each group of students followed an organised but flexible program of integrated activities. Lecturers from all departments visited the Annexe and contributed to the program. Groups of students taking Art, Music, Physical Education and Recreation and Science accompanied by academic staff, also used the Annexe at weekends for programs of specialised activities. The Annexe became an integral part of the College, providing opportunities for sound personal relationships to develop away from the academic setting of the Frankston campus. Portsea Camp became an integral part of the teaching practicum where third year students would run children's camps under supervision.

Lay Lin Oh, a former staff member, recalls weekend vacations at the Portsea Annexe. She retains vivid memories of weekend visits to the Annexe with her family and clearly remembers the kitchen, shower block and accommodation dormitory with bunk beds for 30 students and a separate cabin with a lounge and fireplace which was cosy in the evenings.

The Portsea Annexe was sold around the time of the amalgamation with Monash in 1990. The site is now known as Ramler Mews, apparently named after the Chisholm Council member, and later Deputy Chancellor of Monash, Paul Ramler.

REMEMBERING 1975 – SERVING THE BEST INTEREST OF THE MAJORITY

1975 is remembered in Australian history for the dismissal on 11 November by the Governor-General, Sir John Kerr, of the Whitlam Labour Government. This event almost stopped the nation; it caused great controversy at the time and has remained an issue of contention ever since.

The Government was dismissed by Kerr because of Gough Whitlam's failure to secure supply and his refusal to resign or recommend a dissolution (Cowen, 2006: 303). There was widespread shock and criticism, as well as support for the Governor-General's action. This event, however, created deep and bitter division in Australian society, a rift that healed slowly over time.

Conflict between individual personalities and the student representative body, the SRC, also emerged during 1975 at Frankston. It was a difficult time. In the pages of *Struan*, members of the SRC spoke out about their troubled year. Dissident individuals and factions had caused havoc. The increase in student numbers and the possibility of an oversupply of teachers appears to have created a degree of uncertainty. Enrolments at the SCV at Frankston reached 1086 (Norris & Partners, 1975). It is conceivable that the political events of the year also unsettled the student body more than they imagined.

Douglas Watson, the Principal, wrote in his annual report in *Struan* that the SRC Executive had served in the best interest of the majority of students in 1975 and that he respected the way they achieved their goal.

The SRC's Vice-President went a little further and warned students that:

> Acting as an individual, not supporting SRC policy and decisions,
> causes conflict, factions and confusion. This occurred in 1975. I hope
> it will not happen to the 1976 Executive (*Struan*, 1975).

The strong message running throughout the 1975 edition of *Struan* was that individualism and factionalism was problematic for the healthy working of a democratically elected SRC.

Notwithstanding the political problems of the year, social events, especially live entertainment, was a major hit. Frankston students enjoyed a stellar line-up of all-time great Australian rock bands performing at the College. Now legendary names such as Ross Ryan, Skyhooks, Ayers Rock, Bushwackers, Richard Clapton, Captain Matchbox and the Whoopee Band, Dingoes and Split Enz all played at Frankston. Lorraine Osborne, a first year student, wrote enthusiastically in *Struan* that:

> In my opinion, we have had a great line up of groups this year, two that immediately come to mind are 'Skyhooks' and 'The Hot City Bump Band' ... so let's keep the flag flying at this college (*Struan*: 1975).

Figure 6 Skyhooks Concert at Frankston 1975
Monash University Archives, MON 1206 State College of Victoria Frankston Yearbooks

Highlights of the year for students also included a huge variety of sporting activities, music, recreation clubs, theatre and the first SCV Frankston feminist Women's Activist Group was formed.

More so than any other year in its history, students at Frankston were politically active during 1975 – whether individually, as a radical faction, as part of the SRC, or protesting politely in the pages of *Struan* – student opinion of all shades was made public.

PROGRESSIVE CHANGES IN COURSE OFFERINGS AT FRANKSTON

Frankston was slowly diversifying and expanding its course offerings. Additions to the 1959 courses did not take place until 1968 when the Diploma of Teaching (Primary) was added, and in 1976 the Diploma of Teaching (Early Childhood) commenced. In 1977, the Graduate Diploma in Education (Multicultural Education) was introduced, followed in 1978 by the Diploma of Teaching (Primary) which formed part of the Bachelor of Education. In the same year, the Graduate Diploma in Art Education was offered.

The State College of Victoria's *Annual Report* described the year 1977 as a year 'of frustration and uncertainty'. This uncertainty was intensified by the substitution of annual for triennial funding by the Fraser Government, and by the replacement of the Advanced, Technical and Further Education and the Universities Commissions with the Tertiary Education Commission and its three advisory councils (*Annual Report* 1977:5). The year was also made more difficult for the SCV by the existence of State and Federal Inquiries into the whole field of post-secondary education, the result of which would not be played out for some time. It was the precursor of many disruptive years ahead.

The 1977 *Annual Report* also noted that under the chairmanship of Mr Justice Asche, the Council promoted the future role of the College as a regional college in its submission to the Committee inquiring into Post-Secondary Education. One result of the submission to the inquiry was the decision to encourage community members to become more aware of the staff and student population at the College, and in particular, to utilise facilities on campus. Invitations were extended to local groups to visit the College and meet members of the Council and staff. Additionally, a wide range of evening classes and lectures was offered for members of the local community. These proved very successful and, together with the provision of courses for the up-grading of teachers' qualifications and in-service courses for practising teachers, the College fulfilled its charters as a more comprehensive institution in its service to the community (*Annual Report* 1977: 23).

The Victorian Teachers' Union boycotted the supervision of student teachers in schools in 1977 and this meant that school experience for pre-service students was difficult. However, the good relationship the College had built up with the local schools enabled limited training to take place.

Doug Watson, the first Principal of the State College of Victoria at Frankston, retired in March 1977 and the leadership of the College passed to Dr Graham Trevaskis, BA, B.Ed., MA, Ed.D., TPTC, formerly Principal of the SCV at Ballarat. Under his direction a new organisational structure was proposed, debated and endorsed by staff and Council. It took effect from 1978. The College was also preparing to teach some of its courses away from McMahons Road in primary and secondary schools, teaching centres and colleges of technical and further education. These moves aimed to service the needs of part-time students through studies being offered externally as well as after normal school hours.

The year 1980, in which the College celebrated 21 years as a post-secondary education institution, proved to be difficult and dramatic. The recommendations of the Victorian Post-Secondary Education Commission foreshadowed the fact that Frankston would in the future become more than an institution to train teachers and would evolve into a multi-disciplinary institute of higher education (*Annual Report* 1980: 3). Serving the region, however, remained its first priority, and this was reiterated by Trevaskis in the annual reports from 1977 to 1981. Additional courses were offered: in 1979 the Graduate Diploma in Educational Administration and the Graduate Diploma in Educational Studies (Learning Difficulties in Language and Mathematics) and in 1980 the Graduate Diploma in Music Therapy.

The name and structure of the College was soon to change. The increased and changing needs of the local residents for post-secondary education were the basis of this move. In May 1981 the Minister of Education, Alan Hunt, announced the recommendations of the Victorian Post-Secondary Education Commission. They included the dissolution of the Council of SCV Frankston; that Caulfield Institute of Technology accept responsibility for the provision of advanced education in the Frankston region by establishing a campus there; and that a 1984 target total student load for the Caulfield Institute of Technology (on both the Caulfield and Frankston campuses) be 4600, of whom 800 were to be located at Frankston. The die was set. Frankston, which had remained a single-purpose college of advanced education for 22 years, was being forced to amalgamate with another institution, diversify and expand to become a multi-disciplinary institution of higher or advanced education. In 1973, when he attended the opening of the George Jenkins Theatre, the then Education Minister and Deputy Premier, Lindsay Thompson, projected that the college could develop into a complex with between 2000 and 3000 students. He saw the strength and vitality that was evident at the College at the time. His prescient words became reality more than thirty years later.

Gertrude (Trudy) Kentish, BA, B.Ed., Dip.Phys.Ed., TPTC

Gertrude Kentish was one of the first four appointments to the Frankston Teachers' College. She had attended Bendigo Teachers' College and began teaching as a student teacher at Kangaroo Flats before relocating to Natya West in the Mallee as head teacher. Following this, she attended Melbourne Teachers' College, gaining her TPTC and was appointed to the Physical

Education staff for the swimming season and afterwards to Leonard's Hill State School as head teacher. After being granted a National Fitness Scholarship to study physical education at the University of Melbourne, she was appointed lecturer in Physical Education at Ballarat Teachers' College. Before being posted to Geelong Teachers' College as PE lecturer, she was seconded by the Education Department to the British Commonwealth Occupation Force in Japan, and taught children of British, American and Australian servicemen at Army Headquarters in the Inland Sea for 12 months. On returning to Australia she took up her position at Geelong Teachers' College, during which time she studied at night for her BA, later Dip. Ed. and B. Ed. Trudy then spent a year on exchange in England as a staff member of Goldsmiths College of the University of London.

As an inaugural staff member at Frankston Teachers' College, Trudy was Senior Woman Lecturer in charge of the Social Science Department. In 1970 she was appointed Vice-Principal, and was Acting Principal in 1971 and 1973.

Miss Kentish attended the education section of the United Nations International Women's Year Conference in Mexico City in 1975. She was also an active member of the SRC, the Victorian Women Graduates Association, Soroptimist International, National Trust of Australia (Victoria), Frankston Music Society and the Monturna Golf Club.

Trudy Kentish retired from the State College of Victoria at Frankston on her 60th birthday in January 1981. As her students acknowledged, her long career as a senior teacher and administrator, demonstrated to women that it was possible to excel in senior teaching appointments.

Figure 7 Miss Gertrude Kentish
Monash University Archives, MON 1206, State College of Victoria Yearbooks

5. AMALGAMATION CHALLENGES: CHISHOLM INSTITUTE OF TECHNOLOGY – 1982 TO 1990

The social and political climate in Australia began to change in the 1980s. In 1982, successive Liberal/Country Party governments had been in power in Victoria for 27 years. However, the Premier, Lindsay Thompson, was defeated in the April 1982 election and replaced by Labour leader, John Cain. The Federal Liberal Government, which had been led by Malcolm Fraser since November 1975, was replaced in March 1983 by the R J (Bob) Hawke Labour government.

In 1983 Australia was riding on the crest of a wave of patriotism and pride in its achievements: *Australia II*, skippered by Monash graduate, John Bertrand, had won the 1983 Americas Cup challenge. At the same time, the country was experiencing one of the worst droughts in its history. Victoria and South Australia were devastated by the Ash Wednesday Fires on 16 February 1983, killing 62 people. At a time when unemployment levels, inflation and interest rates were at record highs, the tertiary and university sectors were being reformed despite limited federal and state government funding.

Following the Post-Secondary Education Commission's recommendations, the Caulfield Institute of Technology and the State College of Victoria at Frankston were directed to amalgamate. The tone of annual and internal reports alludes to an unenthusiastic union. Putting on their best face, Chisholm Institute of Technology's *First Annual Report 1982*, detailed the amalgamation and its challenges. The aims of the report were twofold: first, to 'acknowledge the continuity of educational activities through the awards and courses' at Chisholm; second to 'show how Chisholm assessed its inheritance in order to shape new directions and give new emphasis to the activities and community services' (*First Annual Report* 1982: 1). P D Leary, then Assistant Chief Officer of Britain's Council for National Academic Awards, was appointed Foundation Director of the Chisholm Institute of Technology and took up the appointment in January 1983.

The new multi-disciplinary tertiary institution, named the Chisholm Institute of Technology, opened in 1982. It offered studies in seven schools located on two campuses – Caulfield and Frankston. The six Chisholm schools located at Caulfield were Applied Science, Art and Design, Computing and Information Systems, the David Syme Business School, Engineering, and Social and Behavioural Science. The seventh, at Frankston, was based on the teacher education activities of the former SCV at Frankston. One of the first tasks for the amalgamated Chisholm Institute of Technology was the development of the Frankston campus as quickly as possible.

Figure 8 Laying foundations of General teaching building at Frankston Campus 1986
Monash University Archives, IN3125

From the reminiscences of some former State College staff, the amalgamation was, at the time, seen as a takeover. However, despite their possibly disgruntled state, the staff got on with the business of teaching. Notwithstanding negative attitudes, oral testimony clearly demonstrates the close relationships between staff and the commitment to teaching that remained in place during each phase of its history. Bob Greaves, who lectured at Frankston from 1968 to 2006 recalls proudly that the relationship between staff was close and students formed life-long relationships at the College (Greaves, May 2008).

By 1985, the number of enrolled students had increased. At Caulfield 5363 were enrolled and at Frankston the enrolments had increased to 1248 (*Annual Report* 1985: 4).

Plans dating back to 1978 to include nursing in the curriculum began to be realised in 1985 when it was announced that a new building for Nurse Education would be constructed and a student intake of 90 would commence in the 1987 academic year.

By 1987, Chisholm Institute of Technology was the third largest of Victoria's colleges of advanced education with an enrolment of around 6500 students. At Frankston, courses were offered in the Schools of Education and Nursing, the School of Art and Design, the David Syme Business School, the School of Social and Behavioural Studies, and in the Division of Information Technology (*Handbook*, 1987).

Teaching innovation continued at Frankston. A two-day in-service program for teachers in the southern metropolitan region in was run in 1989. Programs were offered to about 400 teachers under the four headings of social issues, assessment and evaluation, technology and its role in the primary school, and curriculum issues. One of the benefits of the workshop, according to In-Service Coordinator Tom Hill, was that the scheme enabled teachers and Chisholm staff to establish a closer relationship and understanding in a shared work environment (*Chisholm Gazette*, July 1989: 17).

THE DAWKINS PLAN AND ANOTHER MERGER

> The traditional universities will be forced to raise funds from the corporate sector and from the marketing of their programmes to overseas students. Whether or not they will succeed in this only time will tell. But the cosy and sheltered world of the academic in the traditional universities will be shattered ... the Dawkins Plan has forced mergers on the traditional universities (Gupta, 1990).

In his article, 'The Dawkins Higher Education Plan: Its rationale and implications', Desh Gupta reviews the Dawkins plan and the consequences as he saw them for the future of universities and CAEs. The need to raise funds by marketing education to overseas students has been a significant factor in the development of Monash University.

Figure 9 Tree planting at Frankston by Monash Chancellor, Sir George Lush, 1989
Monash University Archives, IN3195

John Dawkins, Minister for Employment, Education and Training from 1987–91 in the third Hawke government, set about reforming the education sector in the late 1980s. Dawkins' 'Higher education, a policy discussion paper' set out methods of increasing enrolments and output of tertiary qualified students in the years 1987–2001 (Dawkins 1987). This was achieved by changing the funding structure to traditional universities and colleges of advanced education. The Australian Research Council (ARC) was created as part of Dawkins policy to 'claw back resources from the traditional universities of 4 per cent of operating grants' and to make funds available, on a competitive basis, and in terms of national priorities, to the traditional universities as well as CAEs (Gupta, 1990: 159).

Under the Dawkins plan, the forty-one CAEs and twenty universities which existed in 1989 were expected to be reduced, through mergers, to thirty universities. This would involve the subsuming of the CAEs into the established universities, mergers between CAEs, and the conversion of some CAEs into universities through a period of sponsorship by the more established universities (Gupta: 159). Dawkins promoted many benefits to come from his scheme, not least, the result of the introduction of a new funding scheme through the Higher Education Contribution Scheme or HECS. The change of status from CAEs to universities was seen as a great gain for academics and students at institutions such as the Chisholm Institute of Technology.

It was therefore no surprise when it was reported in 1989 in the *Chisholm Gazette* that Chisholm and Monash, 'two of Victoria's premier higher educational institutions' had agreed to a merger process leading to the establishment on 1 July 1990 of the second biggest university in Australia (*Chisholm Gazette*, July 1989: 3). The 1990 *Handbook* spelled out the benefit for students:

> [A] diverse unified and more equitable higher education system serving Melbourne's eastern and south-eastern regions; a major expansion of higher education opportunities within Monash University, with a greater range of available disciplines and awards; improved flexibility of subject choice and better provisions for transfer of credit within and between disciplines; and a broadening of student services and facilities for teaching and research (*Handbook*, 1990: 2).

The dawning of another new era awaited the staff and students of the Caulfield and Frankston campuses of Chisholm Institute of Technology. Illustrative of the attitude of some of the staff to another impending 'merger', the front cover of the July edition of the *Chisholm Gazette* was emblazoned with the word 'SOLD!!!'.

Robert (Bob) Greaves, OAM

Bob Greaves was appointed to the Frankston Teachers' College in 1968 after serving 18 months as a seconded lecturer in Art at Melbourne Teachers' College. During the turbulent years of the Chisholm administration, Bob also taught ceramics at the Caulfield campus, sharing his time between Art and Design and Education. However his primary interest was in Children's Art and he returned to the Education Faculty at Frankston on a full time basis.

Bob's interest later spread to Technology studies: as he says 'making stuff not the IT that is "Technology" today'. This interest grew from the need to develop creative thinking and the British Craft, Design and Technology model of an amalgamation of science and art.

In Bob's later years at Monash he filled an administrative role as Campus Coordinator for the Faculty of Education, as well as art education teacher. He always regarded himself as a 'Pracademic'. Bob remained at the Frankston campus, seeing it undergo the various transformations as Chisholm and then Monash, until his retirement from Monash University in 2006.

In January 2007 Bob was awarded the Medal of the Order of Australia for service to the community through the provision of therapeutic play activities for children in hospital, and to education.

6. AND NOW WE ARE MONASH UNIVERSITY

In the academic year 1990, new students enrolled, and existing students re-enrolled, under Chisholm regulations. The *Monash University (Chisholm and Gippsland) Act 1990* came into force on 1 July 1990: Chisholm courses became Monash courses and Chisholm staff and students became Monash staff and students.

Both staff and students recognised the difference in status. Monash University had a budget of about $200 million a year and an enrolment of nearly 30,000 students. The merger agreement read:

> The merger of these two institutions will result in a significantly enlarged and changed Monash University capable of both maintaining the reputation of the academic programs currently offered by both institutions and enabling the development of important new academic initiatives that will benefit the community they serve. Such an association will be to the mutual advantage of both institutions by adding to the strengths of existing courses and extending the range of educational opportunities available to students…The bringing together of these interests will generate opportunities for available resources to be used to advantage, providing a better basis of innovation and change (*Handbook*, 1990: 2).

In his Vice-Chancellor's Statement, Professor Mal Logan, AO, reported that Monash had consolidated its standing 'as one of the world's great research universities' and had expanded to the point that it had become 'a large and diverse institution of enormous potential' (*Annual Report*, 1991). The enlarged university, which in 1991 had merged with the Gippsland Institute of Advanced Education, was 'uniquely positioned to move ahead as an innovative, outward-looking, enterprising institution' (*Annual Report*, 1991: 1). One further merger which took place in 1992 was with the Victorian College of Pharmacy; it became the Faculty of Pharmacy and is now known as the Parkville Campus. In 1994 the Berwick campus was established, and this completed the suite of six suburban and regional Australian Monash university campuses.

The links between Monash University and the staff and students of Frankston Teachers' College date back to 1961 and Monash University's first enrolment of students. P J Hanna, who described himself as a 'student in training' wrote to the Secretary of the Education Department on 2 March 1961 seeking leave on the afternoon of 3 March 1961. He wrote: 'I wish permission for leave on the afternoon of Friday 3rd March 1961.

The leave concerns an appointment at Monash University for admission to a science course of which I wish to do part-time' (VPRS 10536/P/0000 Unit 19). Subsequent students and teachers, such as Max Gillies and others, made their way to Clayton campus for the same reason.

Figure 10 Aerial view of Monash University Peninsula Campus, 1990
Monash University Archives, IN6692

The expanded Monash University's objectives for the future naturally included research and teaching; however, in 1991 it was announced that two additional aims were added into the mix: one was the internationalisation of the University; the other was the introduction of new and technological modes of delivery. Peninsula Campus would become involved in both of these initiatives (*Annual Report* 199: 1).

February 1998 witnessed the opening of the Monash University Malaysia campus, this was followed in September 1998 by the announcement that Monash University had become a member of the prestigious Group of Eight (GO8). Membership of the G08, whose policy is to maximise the economic, social and cultural benefits to the Australian community of higher education has informed Monash's expansion and internationalisation policies. In 2001, a South African campus of Monash University was opened, and later that year, the Prato Centre opened in Italy. By 2001 Monash had become the multi-campus multi-disciplinary university that it is today.

CREATING A NICHE FOR PENINSULA CAMPUS

As Monash University, the Peninsula Campus expanded in the years following the Chisholm/Monash merger. By 1992 courses such as Computing and Information Technology were extended to Peninsula Campus which also offered courses in Art and Design, Business and Economics, Education, and Nursing. However, Monash Peninsula Campus was at a low ebb, and appears to have been, at best, operating in a holding pattern during this time.

Plans for the future expansion and internationalisation of the multi-campus Monash were outlined in the draft document, *Leading the Way: Monash Plan, 1998–2002* (1997). The plan revealed that the viability of the Peninsula Campus was threatened. The long period of decline and the fact that limited quantifiable research was being undertaken were seriously hindering the future of the campus. Staff and students rallied and in July, Peninsula staff representatives, Cathi Lewis and Sam Kandil, presented their views on the *Monash Plan* to Council. They proposed that the cuts to Peninsula Campus would jeopardise the future of the campus and that their aim in attending the Council meeting was to highlight the positive ways that Peninsula Campus could contribute to the future of Monash University.

Together they made their case. They suggested that major decisions relating to the campus should be postponed until a more formalised campus direction was determined; and that Council consider forming a sub-committee to guide future development. The representatives also submitted that some of the perceived disadvantages of the campus should be seen instead as advantages. Some of the points made echoed the very reasons the Education Department had chosen the Frankston site for a college forty years earlier, in 1957:

- that the Peninsula Campus was outside inner Melbourne but on the edge of a growth corridor
- that the area was serviced by a good public transport system and has access to all types of industry
- that the location of the campus lifted the educational profile of the area and the campus is considered by many local residents as a community resource
- that students have access to good quality accommodation within easy reach of amenities.

The representatives outlined the extent of concern expressed by both staff and students at Peninsula to the proposed cuts. Council was advised that a petition, signed by 5000 concerned staff and students, was testament to their concern. Protests had been held in Frankston to alert the community to the possible reduction of the campus.

The Vice-Chancellor, Professor David Robinson, responded to the issues raised by the Peninsula staff. At the outset, he noted that, while change would be inevitable at Peninsula, the enthusiasm of staff would be mobilised to help define the role of the campus within the greater Monash community. He advised that David Phillips, Special Advisor to the Vice-Chancellor and the Deans of faculties, would assist with the development of a new and appropriate portfolio of programs for the campus by mid-1998. At the same time, the revised planning process would identify an appropriate research focus for the campus and ways to best utilise the physical infrastructure at Peninsula. To the pertinent question of why the University could not create similar conditions for excellence at Peninsula as had been achieved at other campuses, the Vice-Chancellor responded that clarification of the role and focus of Peninsula Campus would be 'a specific and differentiated focus'. This, he said, would 'assist in creating an environment where the pursuit of excellence was an integral part of all campus activities'. He went on to highlight some of the differences between Peninsula and Gippsland campuses and noted that Gippsland had a clear vision of its role within the community and considered its programs and research profile within those parameters (Council Minutes 4/1997). For Monash Council's purposes, Peninsula was required to articulate a clearer vision of itself and its place within both Monash and the local regional community.

As a result of the Council meeting, Peninsula staff and administration concentrated on planning the new direction of the campus. In November, when the Academic Board met, John White, Director of the Caulfield and Peninsula campuses, presented his report, *The Development of Peninsula Campus*. The Vice-Chancellor advised the Board that he had accepted the principles of the report which was in its initial stages of implementation (Academic Board 8/97).

Community engagement, together with innovation and internationalisation, became a major focus of Monash University in the late 1990s – and has remained so. This component of the Peninsula Campus's activities is possibly greater in 2008 than it has ever been. However, a review of annual reports of the Frankston Teachers' College, State College of Victoria and Chisholm Institute of Technology clearly demonstrates the strong connection each institution had with its local community. For example, one of the lasting benefits of the State College of Victoria's interaction with the local community resulted in a donation to the campus Library of a rare music collection by local resident Vera Florence Bradford, Mus.D.Dip. It contained scores and sheet music, librettos and histories of music. In her honour it was named the Vera Bradford Music Collection, and became part of the Library's special collection (*Annual Report 1978*: 22). Over the past twenty years, material from other donors has been added to the Vera Bradford Collection which now also contains donations from Peninsula music groups, bands of the defence forces and other materials purchased by Monash University Library.

The Library has always been an integral part of a student's life. In the 1990s libraries had to cope with the rapid rate of technological change and at the Peninsula Library, staff had to cope with new technology, staffing levels and user needs. Libraries were no longer simply places which housed books, journals, maps and teaching aids. In 1995 approval was given for a library to be constructed on the site occupied by the student hostel. This building was demolished and the new library was completed in 1997 and opened in February 1998. The Library was designed to sit comfortably within its environment and complement the native flora prevalent at the Peninsula Campus while providing excellent Information Technology facilities.

Figure 11 Peninsula Library 2008
Photographer: Sue Webb, Monash University Peninsula Campus

Despite the staff's efforts to redirect the focus of the Peninsula Campus, John White, Campus Director, had witnessed the decline of student numbers from the mid-1990s. At a meeting of the Faculty of Information Technology in November 2001, he addressed this pressing issue which he would take to all faculties. While a review of the campus activities and University strategic planning had been in progress for five years, White argued that greater research activity and internationalisation was still necessary. Group of Eight universities were required to research, and at that stage Peninsula Campus still lacked a focused research policy. The future direction of the campus, he argued, lay with individual faculties increasing their student numbers. Faculties considered their options.

Figure 12 The late John White, Director of Peninsula and Caulfield campuses from October 1997 to December 2002
Monash University Archives, IN6738

After many years of working to develop the campus, in 2002 in his final year as Campus Director, the late John White launched the Peninsula Hockey Centre. This centre illustrates the commitment of the Peninsula Campus to providing facilities to the local community. The cost was shared between Frankston City Council, Monash University, the Monash Student Union, Mornington Peninsula Shire Council, Sport and Recreation Victoria and local hockey clubs. It is now the home of three hockey clubs and also hosts the Monash Peninsula Seadragons Soccer Club! When it was officially launched in April 2002, then Sport and Recreation Minister, Justin Madden, said the hockey pitch not only provided a much needed resource for sport in the region, it also showed what could be achieved when communities worked together. The Hockey Centre continues to be heavily utilised by local schools as well as by Monash Peninsula students.

Figure 13 Peninsula Campus students, 2008
Photograph: Rachael Martyn 2008, Monash University Peninsula Campus

Professor Phillip Steele, then Associate Dean Development in the Faculty of Information Technology, was appointed Academic Director Berwick and Peninsula campuses in 2003. He was responsible for leading the development and integration of teaching, research and community engagement activities at both campuses.

In 2003, he established the Peninsula Education Precinct to explore ways of establishing links between secondary schools, TAFE and university. The Education Precinct has run successfully for five years. It provides enhanced educational opportunities for students in the southern and south-eastern suburbs of Melbourne, and the Frankston and Mornington Peninsula region. Membership of the Education Precinct includes Monash University Peninsula Campus, Chisholm Institute of TAFE, the Department of Education and Training, Frankston City Council, representation from local Frankston secondary schools, Mornington Peninsula Local Learning and Employment Network and the Mornington Peninsula Shire Council. The partners retain their own educational identity and focus, while collaborating closely with each other to break down institutional and sectoral barriers.

The Precinct's major objectives are to create a framework for the identification and management of innovative, regionally specific, educational pathways designed to maximise learning opportunities. It also aims to contribute to the intellectual, economic and cultural development of the region by collaborative arrangements between educational providers, industry and relevant communities. For example, one popular initiative developed since 2002 are the VCE revision lectures. Enrolment in these revision lectures has increased since 2004 from 300 to 1100 in 2007. Campus Manager, Sue Webb believes the appeal of these lectures is widespread and growing, and local students relish the opportunity to spend time on the university campus as well as gain tremendously from the revision process.

Phillip Steele's second major initiative, in 2003–4, was a bid to create a 'health precinct' at Peninsula Campus.

Figure 14 Professor Phillip Steele
Monash University

The Health Precinct was developed by Professor Leon Piterman (Deputy Dean Faculty of Medicine, Nursing and Health Sciences), Associate Professor Tony Luff (Associate Dean Teaching, Faculty of Medicine, Nursing and Health Sciences, Mr Brian Ruck (Consultant) and Professor Steele. The group argued that the health precinct would encourage close collaboration between the academic units located at Monash Peninsula, Chisholm TAFE Frankston and the nearby health agencies. It was also proposed the precinct would provide an exciting framework for collaboration, teaching, research, professional development, student placement, and resource and information sharing.

In 2005 the Faculty of Education made a decision to relocate its Sport and Outdoor Recreation programs from the Gippsland to the Peninsula Campus with programs commencing at Peninsula in 2006. The motivation for this move was the prospect of improved teaching and learning facilities; the programs also fitted well with the campus' new health and wellbeing theme.

Together with the Education Precinct, a Health Precinct was considered a further factor in differentiating Peninsula from Monash's other suburban campuses. Monash welcomed the arrival of the multi-disciplinary Peninsula Health Precinct in 2005. Health and wellbeing programs are now offered by the Education Faculty, the Faculty of Business and Economics and the Faculty of Medicine, Nursing and Health Sciences. Bachelor degrees in Nursing, Midwifery, Emergency Health (Paramedics), Occupational Therapy, Physiotherapy, Health Science and Social Work are all located at Peninsula.

After considerable thought and planning by campus administration and faculties, the Peninsula Campus has embraced a distinguishable research program. Though it covers a diverse range of areas, the emerging theme is predominantly one of health and wellbeing, exemplifying the theme expressed by the Peninsula Campus in the *Monash Directions 2025* document, 'Peninsula: Understanding successful living' (*Monash Direction 2025*: 2005: 20). Another key theme that all academic areas focus on is best practice in education. Research into areas including curriculum development, student learning and expectations, the role of the 'hands on' experience in tertiary education and the impact of professional education, demonstrate how research and teaching skills can merge. There are currently approximately 100 Higher Degrees by Research students enrolled at the Peninsula Campus.

All faculties now have a strong research program. The Department of Community Emergency Health and Paramedic Practice has a strong research focus on trauma and pre-hospital care. This centre is particularly active in collaborative research with the Victorian Trauma Foundation. Staff in the Faculty of Business and Economics conduct research into many areas, with key research strengths in international business strategy and business education. The Faculty of Education has a particular focus on research into early childhood and primary education, and sport and outdoor recreation, and the profile of the Department of Health Science is predominantly in the public health-social sciences field. A unique blending of social health sciences and bio-science creates opportunities for multi-paradigm and mixed method research partnerships. The School of Nursing incorporates research into models of care in a range of nursing settings including palliative care, midwifery, acute clinical care and mental health. New to the Peninsula Campus in 2005, research in the field of occupational therapy (OT) explores issues including forensic OT, young people in nursing homes, paediatric OT and professional accreditation. Physiotherapy research currently focuses on the risk of pulmonary complications following upper abdominal surgery.

In the ten years since the major threat to the viability of the Peninsula Campus, research has flourished and forms a major component of the various precincts established since 2001. The previous tension that existed between provision of teaching and undertaking research appears to have been resolved.

Mathew Keates, MONSU Peninsula President 2008

The current Monash University Student Union (MONSU) President, Mathew Keates, has recently graduated B.Bus.Comm. He enrolled in a Bachelor of Business and Commerce degree in 2004. He attended Banking and Finance units at Caulfield Campus as part of his degree, but he chose to study at Peninsula because of the people and culture at the campus. He says:

> As Peninsula is one of Monash's smaller campuses, being able to walk around campus where you know all the faces, feeling comfortable in all your classes, building strong relationships with your lecturers and tutors and feeling a real sense of belonging was really important to the whole university experience. I found these particular aspects were more prominent at the Peninsula Campus, more so than any other campus.

Now that he's completed his degree, and in his role as MONSU President, Mathew is enjoying the opportunity of providing students with 'an unforgettable university experience'. His tasks relate to planning, organising and implementing Student Council activities, and he finds this very rewarding.

Mathew has noticed the campus has changed physically in four years. 'Peninsula has developed into such a beautiful campus with one of the main changes being the landscaping out the front of the Library which has turned this area into a great place for students to be able to hang out while at the same time becoming an informal learning space'.

7. CONCLUSION

When the Frankston Teachers' College opened its doors on 12 February 1959, it was an institution which reflected the Australian population at the time. Surnames of both students and staff were still predominantly Anglo-Australian. College documents show an initial enrolment of 109 students (VPRS 10536/P/0000 Unit 19).

Monash University Peninsula Campus now offers a range of courses to local as well national and international students. The most recently published official statistics, *Pocket Statistics 2007*, indicate that the total enrolment at Peninsula Campus in 2006 was 3314. In 2008 it has risen to nearly 3500 with over 200 staff. Nearly 30 per cent of the domestic students at the campus come from the Frankston-Mornington Peninsula region. Though this number is thirty times greater than the initial enrolment of only 109 students in 1959, the female:male ratios remain similar:

- 68.8% females; 31.2% males
- 63.8% full-time; 21.3% part-time and 14.8% external students
- 11.6% international (overseas fee paying)
- average age of students is 27.2 years.

Other statistics provide a broader picture of the Peninsula student:

- 288 school leavers
- 678 new to higher education
- 10 of Aboriginal descent
- 841 born overseas
- 2,930 Australian citizens
- of the Australian residents, 88.9% spoke English at home while of the 384 international students, 11.5% speak English at home.

It is a diverse group and is indicative of the current make-up of our Australian population.

Much like the first Principal of Frankston Teachers' College, the current Campus Manager, Sue Webb, and Academic Director, Professor Phillip Steele, both believe that a university experience is more than simply attending lectures. Despite the cessation of Voluntary Student Unionism in 2006, the campus continues to offer extra-curricular activities for both students and staff. The Student Representative Council continues to encourage student participation and debate. Sporting, social and cultural activities still form part of campus life.

When the *Monash University Act 1958* established and incorporated the University, section 5(d) of the *Act* specified the provision of facilities for University education throughout Victoria by the affiliation of existing educational institutions (*Monash University Act 1958*). A link was established between Frankston Teachers' College and the University and subsequent institutions. Fifty years after the establishment of the Frankston Teachers' College, and eighteen years after it became a Monash University campus, Peninsula is well established as an important and unique component of Monash's multi-campus university.

Throughout its four phases – as Frankston Teachers' College, State College of Victoria at Frankston, Chisholm Institute of Technology Frankston Campus and now as Monash University Peninsula Campus – the overriding theme to emerge has been that a strong sense of belonging quickly develops and creates a solid bond between students, academics and staff, emphasising the value of a small campus to both teaching and learning. What is perhaps equally striking is that, from the outset, the campus has engaged with its local community, and continues to do so. It now offers a suite of programs from all faculties that are aligned with local industry needs. It provides local tertiary access to local students in a region with levels of university participation and university qualified residents below the Victorian average. Through its affiliation with its various local communities – social, sporting, cultural, academic and educational – Monash University Peninsula Campus can claim that it is very much 'in the world' (*Monash Directions 2025*: 20).

Monash Peninsula Campus has made a distinct name for itself in the region as a multi-disciplinary institute of higher education, and will, it is hoped, continue to do so for a further 50 years.

REFERENCES

PRIMARY SOURCES

INTERVIEWS

Kate Boyle, 14 March 2008
Greg Brown, 9 May 2008
Max Gillies, AM, 27 April 2008
Robert Greaves, 22 May 2008
Paul Jennings, 20 May 2008
Matthew Keates, 22 May 2008
Phillip Steele, 9 May 2008
Sue Webb, 9 May 2008

PUBLICATIONS

Ascolta, 1975–77
Chisholm Institute of Technology Handbook, 1982–1990
Chisholm Institute of Technology Manual, 1982–90
Frankston Teachers' College Handbook, 1959–92
Monash University Annual Reports and Handbooks, 1990–2005
Monash University (Chisholm and Gippsland) Act 1990
Nostrum, 1971–74
Struan, 1960–1975
State College of Victoria Act 1972
State College of Victoria at Frankston Handbook, 1972–81
Through Our Eyes, 1970–71
Monash University Act 1958 No. 6184

ARCHIVAL MATERIAL

Monash University Archives – MON918 and MON 1089, State College of Victoria at Frankston, MON625, Academic Secretariat, MON 1088, Annual Reports, MON 165, Council Minutes, *Leading the Way: Monash Plan 1998–2002* (1997), John White, *The Development of Peninsula Campus* (1997), *Monash Directions 2025* (2005).
Public Record Office Victoria, Education Department, VPRS 10536/P/0000 Unit 19, VPRS 3853, VA437

SECONDARY SOURCES

City of Greater Dandenong History. Available from:
    http://www.greaterdandenong.com/Documents.asp?ID=2645&Title=History.
Compton, Steve. 2008. The Bunurong People. Available from:
    http://www.basscoast.vic.gov.au/files/499_BunurongPeople.pdf.
Cowen, Zelman. 2006. *The Memoirs of Zelman Cowen: A Public Life*, Carlton South: Melbourne University Publishing.
Garden, Don. 1982. *The Melbourne Teacher Training Colleges*, Richmond: Heinemann Educational Australia.
Gupta, Desh. 1990. 'The Dawkins Higher Education Plan: its Rationale and Implications' in *Higher Education Quarterly*, Vol. 44, No. 2, Spring 1990, pp. 154–162.
Inglis, Andrea. 1999. *Beside the Seaside*, Carlton South: The Miegunyah Press.
Parliamentary Handbook of the Commonwealth of Australia, 26th edition 1993. Canberra: Commonwealth of Australia.
Selleck, R J W. 1998. 'Education' in Graeme Davison, John Hirst, Stuart Macintyre (eds) *The Oxford Companion to Australian History*, Melbourne: Oxford University Press.

INDEX

amalgamations, 23, 25–7
Boyd, George WD, 10
Caulfield Institute of Technology, 23, 25
Chisholm Institute of Technology, 25, 26, 28, 30
Chisholm Institute of Technology Frankston Campus, 25–7
community engagement, 22, 33, 35, 41
Dawkins Plan, 27–8
Dignam, Thomas J, 10
Eunson, Warwick, 10–11, 15, 16–17
Frankston Teachers' College, creation of, 9–10
Fry, Alwyn H, 10
George Jenkins Theatre, 16, 19
Gillies, Max, AM, 14–15, 30
Greaves, Robert (Bob), OAM, 26, 29
Hanna, PJ, 30
Hart, Peter, 13
Hill, Tom, 27
Jenkins, George A, 16, 18
Kandil, Sam, 32
Keates, Mathew, 38–9
Kentish, Gertrude F, 10, 23–4
Lewis, Cathi, 32
Logan, Professor Mal, AO, 30
Luff, Associate Professor Tony, 37
Lush, Sir George, 27
mergers, 27–31
Monash University, mergers and expansion, 28–31

Monash University Peninsula Campus, 31, 35
  defining a role for, 32–3, 41
Oh, Lay Lin, 19–20
Osborne, Lorraine, 21
Pappas, George, 19
Peninsula Education Precinct, 36–7
Peninsula Health Precinct, 37
Peninsula Hockey Centre, 35
Peninsula Library, 34
Phillips, David, 33
Piterman, Professor Leon, 37
Portsea Annexe, 19–20
research programs, 33, 34–5, 37–8
Reynolds, Margaret, 14
Robinson, Professor David, 33
Ruck, Brian, 37
State College of Victoria at Frankston, 18, 23, 25
Steele, Professor Phillip, 36, 37, 40
Struan (publication), 10, 13–14, 16, 20
student activism, 13–14, 19, 20
student enrolments, 10, 15, 26, 34, 40
Student Representative Council, 13, 20, 40
teachers' unions, 12, 22
Trevaskis, Dr Graham, 22, 23
Vera Bradford Music Collection, 33–4
Vincent, Dr Frank R, 9
Watson, Douglas, 18, 20, 22
Webb, Sue, 37, 40
White, John, 33, 34, 35